The

DEATH

of the

Tip

ISBN 978-0-557-79117-0

Printed in the United States of America
First Edition, First Printing, October 2010
Business and Money – Professional and Education

Tip. Content. Page

Dedication
Acknowledgments
Overview

DEDICATION

I dedicate this book to every professional who works amiably with the general public.

ACKNOWLEDGEMENTS

My immense gratitude to the following people who helped me along this course: First, my mother, my favorite girl, my Editor, and my biggest cheerleader; she was there to read, edit and add her special brand of wit and sarcasm to this content. Thanks, Mom! Secondly, my dearest friend Jaiya, I appreciate you for encouraging me to speak out in words, and for providing the outline that made this leap of faith practical. I will always treasure our exhaustive conversations. And lastly but most importantly, to the Creator of all living things, who birthed this voice inside of me and gave me the heart and ability to write and share my findings with readers. I am eternally blessed by God's presence in my life.

Many thanks also go out to the actual consumers who provided feedback on their personal experiences. Most chose to remain anonymous but for the others willing to be "pen-pointed" –Elizabeth Ann, Tonta Draper, David Sampson – I appreciate you standing behind your truth. Your words will help us on this journey. Again, I thank you for lending your voice and allowing me to transport the message.

OVERVIEW

On one occasion or another, every human being has considered giving a *non*-monetary tip in some form or fashion. The question is "Why?" This book is the answer. It carries the heavy burden placed on the Average Joe and Jill Consumer, and scripts their thoughts to share with business owners and professionals all over the world who are oftentimes unaware of how this barter system is supposed to work; or are unaware of their employee's destructive actions. Whatever the cause, this epidemic called bad customer service seems determined to kill the enjoyment that comes from giving a good tip, maintaining brand loyalty, etc., and has forced us, the customer, to keep our money in our pockets and leave a little note on a napkin instead.

As humans, we are all fallible, and sometimes we have a bad day but whether poor-performed service is given intentionally or accidentally, it has lasting results. Take these scenarios for instance: What if FedEx forgot to deliver your packages on time? You would call UPS the next time. What if The Cheesecake Factory started serving day old cheesecake? You would start patronizing Copeland's Cheesecake Bistro. What if your cellular service would not correct your bill? When your contract was up, you would switch to another, right? What if you are in France and Hermès will not let you into the store during regular business hours? You would go to Gucci and shell out an exorbitant amount of money on clothes and handbags and send the photos of your shopping excursion to Hermes with a card that reads, "Your Loss."

So how does a company show that they don't take their customer's investment in them for granted? That's the answer you will find in this book, because, as a business owner, I know that no one goes into business, invests years of sweat and tears, to lose money. Business-minded people go into business to make profits. Profits they can use to create a better life for them and their families. That's the bottom line. And that is why I have written this book – to help the economy, and get the money circulating again.

This book is not meant to poke fun, although some of the tips are humorous. It is not intended to be preachy, although the message is serious. It is, however, an honest observation over my career in business development and training coupled with personal experiences of what works and what does not, and I believe with all of my heart that if a professional or a corporation uses these tips, they will see an increase in profits in their life and in their bank accounts.

The Death of the Tip is not just a how-to book but it is an operational guide to follow until the practice of superior service develops into a natural response *because* some people don't have it naturally, but everybody can learn.   Aristotle is quoted as saying "that habits, but a long practice, friend, and this becomes men's nature in the end." With 21 days as the approximate time required before a person creates a new behavior pattern, the manageable, laconic daily doses of instruction in this book are easy to exercise, fun to read and when practiced, can result into higher earning potential, improved health and an overall better attitude about your work.

A person who does their job well is worth every dollar, and my intention is to see that every business, employee, vendor, and supplier learns the larger benefit of serving well. I remember my uncle would start with a base rate and then allow the tip to grow based on actual service; he was always fair and overly generous when the person deserved it. However, if you were on the wrong end of the service odometer, you might find George Washington sitting alone. I believe one reason my uncle was such a good steward of his tip was because he had always been in the business of serving, earning several promotions and accolades; he understood how serving others was supposed to work.

The reality is that we have a deadly outbreak that is spreading with the increase of technology. Intimacy is being replaced by a form of efficiency, and many companies have pressed the delete button on their customer service training.

But the masses are crying out, "Your service stinks." It is rotten, and slowly decaying, and it does not have to. The solution is up to you.

So here's the tip. Not the fifteen, eighteen, and now twenty percent gratuity forced upon us or the automatic renewals that take our choice away, but in this book are twenty-one tried and true tips that will help us all have a win-win experience. Tips that will make us a burgeoning economy once again.

From the valet with his hand out to the contractor who hired the hand; from the board room to the front desk; there is always room for improvement, and something for everyone in this book. There is also a bonus chapter dedicated to equipping the customer. This short chapter gives customers proactive tips on what they can do to receive better service.

Customer service training is one of the simplest, most cost effective upgrades your business can make; and it sets you apart for profits over the competition. Because the spirit is willing but the flesh gets weak, I want to help you day-by-day in your attempt to become a better service provider. Therefore, it is my supreme hope that **The Death of the Tip** will encourage you to exhibit grace in your relationships with consumers and customers, and that you will ultimately *resurrect* the validity of the   tip.

The DEATH of the Tip

one percent

KNOW YOUR WORTH

When was the last time you felt appreciated at your job? That long? Never? Well, that has to change – today.

Most books broach the subject of customer service with *all* the importance directed toward the consumer, hence the phrase "customer service" but that philosophy is not totally accurate, in fact it is rather imbalanced. Who says that for the customer to feel satisfied the business owner or employee has to be disregarded? Both supplier and customer need to have a healthy B2B or B2C relationship and it starts with you. In reality, the only way to genuinely appreciate someone else, customers included, requires personal validation and self-confidence. You must examine and know your worth before you can authentically acknowledge someone else.

Here are only a few reasons why you are important. If you are an employee, do you realize that you were hired to take care of two prized possessions: the company's products/services, and their customer? That is big stuff! Do not take it lightly that they choose you. You may have searched for the position, but ultimately they had to make you an offer. Do you happen to remember the details of your interview? Most people don't because they loathed the process so much; they were simply relieved to get out of the hot seat without soaking through their clothes. Well, whether you recall the experience or not, it is guaranteed that the interviewer, who was either an owner, direct supervisor or the human resource manager, took pride in sharing the company's position in the market, their achievements, and the accolades received. You may have considered it bragging, but what they were actually doing was trying to sell you their company; they were in the position to try and impress you and by the looks of things they succeeded. Yes, with all they have accomplished or hope to attain, they still thought enough of you to ask you to become a part of their world of work.

And it did not stop in the interview. After you were selected, someone likely reiterated the company's mission statement, vision and core values during your training, and before they let you fly solo they were convinced that you had the goods to fit into their corporate culture and soar. Whatever good they thought about themselves, they also now thought you could add to that success. That says a lot about you.

Perhaps you have forgotten your worth and maybe you think those around you have forgotten as well, but if you are still collecting a check, then rest assured - you have value to someone other than yourself. Your company would never pay you to sit around and do nothing, at least not for long. So embrace the fact that you bring a unique element to your job and career, and out of many other people interested in your position, you were the one selected to get the job done. That is favor.

If you own the shop, you probably know how important you are. This business could not exist without you, right? Maybe so or maybe not, what is important is that you understand that you are not a slave to your business, either. Although running a company is not all fun and games, it should never be incessant drudgery. Remind yourself of the passion you had to start this operation, revisit your business plan (you should do this monthly anyway) and the prayers you cried during its conception. Your business has a purpose, and your employees and clients are a part of that vision; take time to remember.

Today's Application:

Find your training manual or business plan and review the company's mission statement, vision, core values and your job description. Take pride in the fact that you were chosen to work at this company or to birth this business idea. Be grateful that you are able to earn a wage and then begin to think about what you bring to the job, and all the ways you add to the company's bottom line and the overall economy, and feel good about your accomplishments. Internalize these feelings today.

notes

THE CUSTOMER PAYS

Remember, balance is required to make this relationship work.

Yesterday was about starting with you, and today is about the other half of this story - recognizing the value of the customer. If the title bothers you it may be possible that the world of business and working with people is not well-suited for you, because the title is a statement of truth and is verifiable whether you are a prison guard or the hotel concierge. It also requires most suppliers, employees, and owners, to check their egos at the door. A quote by David Cornwell, a famed sports attorney, stated on Larry King Live, "It's okay if other people think you're God, but you're in trouble if you start believing it." Ego can destroy an otherwise good business model as well.

In my survey on customer service, "How's Your Service?", when asked "Have you ever continued to patronize a business that provided poor customer service?" most of the responses came back "No." Only in cases where a company had a monopoly on a product or service were consumers "forced" to return to poor service providers.

Without customers there is no need for employees, no need for products, no need to operate a business, and there is no need to read this book. A great idea minus anyone to buy the product or service equals zero, zilch, cero, rein, nada; the concept here is understandable, and the math is not only universally basic but irrefutable.

When people stop spending their money as a whole; it results in a recession and we are all affected, but when people stop spending their money with you specifically; it results in depression. It hits you, directly, in the pocket with possibilities of losing your business and the lifestyle it afforded. So eliminate insecurities from the equation and increase your bottom line by giving your best to your customer.

Just as you have patrons, you are also a consumer with a certain level of expectation when you trade your dollars for service. Aren't you glad that someone values your hard-earned money? The same is true for those who barter with you, and when you and your employees get this foundational key, your business will begin to thrive. You will see every potential customer – regardless of race, ethnicity, age, gender or social status - that comes through the door, or calls on the phone, or visits your website, as priceless.

Today's Application:

Begin to treat each customer like they are your first and your last. Imagine if your entire business hinged on your

next customer; how would that affect the service you deliver? Hold that thought and then make that delivery based on whatever you saw in your mind to do, and then do it again for the next customer, and the next, and so on and so on. What are the results? Take note of this experience and share it within your operation, if possible.

"There is only one boss. The customer. And he can fire everybody in the company from the chairman on down, simply by spending his money somewhere else." Sam Walton

"One customer, well taken care of, could be more valuable than $10,000 worth of advertising." Jim Rohn

notes

KNOW YOUR PRODUCT

One evening, I was invited to share in a celebratory occasion with some new friends at a restaurant in downtown Decatur, Georgia, and I must admit that the service provided by Holly, the waitress, made me feel slightly uncomfortable, but not for the reasons you might think. She was just different – energetic, sociable with good timing, but most significantly, she was knowledgeable. It was like she had studied that menu upside down and backwards, and the way she added her personality into the description was like watching a performance on stage where the lines were so well rehearsed that you forgot it was only a play. Seriously, whenever she would complete her spiel, based on our questions about food or drinks, my tablemates and I would look at each other like "is she real?" This young lady was thorough with a capital "T", not perfect, but overall, she provided outstanding customer service. I did not ask her how long she had worked at this particular spot; it couldn't be too long since Leon's Full Service restaurant opened only months prior to our visit, but whatever they do for training deserves a big red **A+.**

It might be frightening in the beginning, but the world could use more Hollys around, and less Hustlers. Holly is a refreshing example of exceptional product knowledge. Who would not prefer the person who gives all the pertinent facts so you can make an informed decision over the guy who just wants you to "Hurry up Lady, and buy something"? Be it a car, health insurance, or a hotdog; give the customer the time *they* need to make a decision. If you have to leave them with their thoughts that is fine too, but never try to snow a person with your lack of knowledge and heightened hustler moves.

How preposterous it is for a consumer to buy or buy-into something when the person sharing the information does not have a clue what they are talking about? They sound good and they may even look good but there is nothing there. Either they try to over-talk you because they do not know or they are looking at you, blankly, to give them the answer. Do yourself a favor, avoid embarrassment and take some time to get familiar with your products.

Do not be the poor guy who is reading specifications to the consumer that they could read for themselves. Consumers are not illiterate, for the most part, they are only untried. A better practice in this scenario is to provide a demonstration or discuss someone else's experience. The bottom line is if an employee or supplier cannot articulate why a purchase should be made then the consumer is going to have a hard time trusting their recommendation. Just imagine if Holly had never participated in the tastings of Leon's assortment of Sweets; she would never have been able to wow us with her interpretation of each dessert.

Since most people work with the general public, it would be wise to learn something from Holly, and become energized aficionados of the products and services you provide. And if you think you know it all, here's a FREE marketing tip - put a new spin on it by learning to describe it from another perspective. Keeping yourselves knowledgeable about your products and services will most assuredly build your confidence, your customer's trust and your profits.

Today's Application:

Pick a product, any product and research it upside down and backwards. Make it your product of the week. It will build your confidence in your products and your customers trust in you.

"To thine own self be true."
Shakespeare

---

notes

four percent

SPEAK

Have you ever walked into a room of people without knowing anyone? If you are not naturally outgoing, it may have felt awkward. Even in a crowd, you might feel self-conscious like everybody is looking at you but no one is speaking to you. Well, today's customer often has this fish-out-of-water sensation when they walk into a store that is not welcoming.

When a customer opens your door, enters your area (retailers), steps to your counter, you should say "hello" and give some verbal indication of when you will be able to serve them. Of all the components mentioned, this one is my biggest pet-peeve because to not speak is at the height of rudeness. Okay, you spent boatloads of money on advertisements in magazines, sent out mailers, emailed them about the latest and greatest, and when the customer shows up (at your request), you ignore them! Aaaghh! Are you kidding me? You invite them to the party and then disregard them when they take the time to show up. Yes, it happens – all the time - from the well known brands to Mom and Pops all over America.

Why is this so hard? It is amazing how many customers are ignored and their presence unacknowledged. This is a basic, if not THE basic rule of customer service. Customers should never feel they are on the defense. The quickest way to counter this emotion is with a greeting. Instantly, the atmosphere changes and becomes pleasant; a nice environment in which to do business.

For those of you who are "feeling the customer out first", a point of advice. When the phone rings, do you pick it up without saying a word? Think of your next introduction the same way you would treat a telephone call: Door opens (customer calls), Customer steps inside (you pick up the receiver), Customer senses you are not prepared to do business (dead silence), Customer leaves (customer hangs up). No one would act like this on a business call. When the call comes in you immediately respond, "Hello, this is (your name), how may I help you?" So why are you screening your potential customers when they come through the door? The same rules of communication apply. Gone should be the days when a person is rightly compelled to leave an establishment feeling like their business is not appreciated.

As a general rule, you want to recognize the patron as soon as they appear in your peripheral vision. If you are fortunate to have a sensory alert then this will be easy for you. Otherwise, if a customer has to speak to you first; there is a problem and you were too late. Even if you cannot serve them right away, still speak, and tell them you will be with them as soon as possible; whatever the case, say something. Moreover, you need to be expecting them, looking for them to come through the door; not so you can pounce on them or talk them to tears, but to graciously acknowledge their arrival. Everyone enjoys being appreciated.

Take a page from most restaurants; they do a great job of welcoming the customer. They are great for hiring a "host" or "hostess" to do nothing more than greet you at the door. Newbies to customer service are churches, especially mega-churches, who are also doing a fabulous job of this with their unmistakable team of "greeters". These volunteers nearly break their necks to speak and shake the hand of everyone who enters the doors of the church, and guess what, they receive no compensation. However, you do. The church borrowed this idea from Sam Walton because it works. A quick, polite greeting speaks volumes.

Today's Application:

Very simply, say "hello" to each and every customer you come in contact with, BEFORE they speak to you.

"Invisible people spend invisible money and that accounts for nothing."
Leah Taylor

---

notes

INCREASE YOUR FACE VALUE

This is the oldest customer service tool in the shed and perhaps that is why it is seldom bypassed for the shinier new technological ways of communicating, but it is time to get back to basics and show those pearly whites. Your greeting is only as good as the tone of your voice. It is not only what you say but how you say it. That is why receptionists and telemarketers are instructed to smile while they are on the phone. Sure no one can see them but any listener can tell whether the caller is warm and fuzzy or cold and crunchy.

People can hear your smile, and if you sound gracious, it reflects well on the company and within the conversation. The same applies when conversing with customers in person. Have a congenial look and it will come through in your voice. Don't worry if your smile is not as infectious as Julia Roberts, few have been bequeathed with such a gift, but let your authentic, natural glow shine through. A smile is always worth the while. Les Brown, famous motivational speaker, says, "the homeliest person looks good when they smile." Moreover, you feel better when you lighten up and allow your gratitude for living to shine through.

And speak clearly. The modern population has the mumbles. What happened to proper pronunciation, stressing the syllables and inflection? Are people speaking less because there is more tweeting and social media that exempts them from the spoken word? It is obvious that some prefer to text than to talk, but texting, emailing, and tweeting should not abandon the need for oral communication and the supplier's ability to talk. Consumers have to understand you (with or without accent). The onus is on the messenger to get his point across, so speak up, speak clearly and do it with a smile.

Today's Application:

Simply smile when speaking to the patrons. ☺

If you are not a naturally, happy-go-lucky person, this could be a slight challenge so I encourage you to think your most positive thoughts (going to the beach, a favorite quote, winning a million dollars) just before approaching a customer or answering the phone. And please practice in the mirror first. (SMILE).

> **"A smile is an inexpensive way to improve your looks." Charles Gordy**

six percent

LISTEN

On occasion, it may feel nice to blurt out the answer before a customer asks the question, but it is actually insensitive. Instead of jumping into sales mode, why not follow that "Hello, how can I help you?" with a pause, and allow the customer the opportunity to speak. By pausing to hear what they have to say, you can gather all sorts of information about them and what their needs are at that moment. If you listen and help them with their original request, then they will be more apt to listen to you stammer on about the latest and greatest deals and specials. Moreover, effective listening will give you the greater benefit of knowing exactly how to up-sale or meet their future needs. Remember, no one likes to be sold but everyone likes to buy.

Furthermore, when you listen, the customer does not lose their voice nor do they have to battle to be heard. This seems to happen on the swing side of the sale with companies who think they have a monopoly (i.e. phone, utilities and cable services). A customer calls with a question about a malfunctioning product and begins to explain the problem, but the representative jumps in, mid-sentence, to solve the problem without fully understanding the complaint. Now the client has to correct the representative and begin the story again. Sure the customer service representative makes a fine point, but it is not the reason for this call. Not every representative is a phone person or compliance friendly. If this is indeed the case then an effective listening training may be in order or the rep may need to look for another career.

Inevitably, after a few rounds of poor communication with the listening-impaired representative, the customer vehemently requests the supervisor. By this time the customer may be offended, especially after that oh, so rude warning that "the supervisor is going to tell you the same thing". If the supervisor is actually this person's peer seated to the left or right of him, well that may be true, but if this is a good supervisor, trained to listen and resolve conflict, then you will never hear the same thing. The truth of the matter is the major difference in the CSR and the Supervisor is their listening skills. A good supervisor is not hot-headed or impatient and will always ask the consumer to explain the problem in order to find ways to satisfy the customer. A good supervisor knows that the solution is found in the complaint.

Although successfully handled, the customer is stuck with a bad taste for the company because what should have taken only moments has lasted far too long. Who is to blame? The hiring manager and the trainer are culpable, on the short list, for not teaching their representatives how to listen.

Today's Application:

When a customer enters the store and you have appropriately greeted them, pause and listen attentively to their response. Then, proceed to help them find whatever it is that they need before pushing your individual (sales or otherwise) agenda. Do not sell anything to a customer; instead show them why they need to buy it.

When a customer calls with a question of concern or to make a complaint, do not attempt to outtalk them or enter into a shouting match.   Simply listen, take notes if necessary, and when they are done, try to solve the problem. You cannot listen to their concern if you are talking.

"I know that you believe you understand what you think I said, but I'm not sure you realize that what you

heard is not what I meant." Robert McCloskey

"To listen well, is as powerful a means of influence as to talk well, and is as essential to all true conversation." Chinese Proverb

---

"Don't try to tell the customer what he wants. If you want to be smart, be smart in the shower. Then get out, go to work and serve the customer!" Gene Buckley

---

PAY ATTENTION

Perhaps you own or work in a storefront and you are following the daily plan and offered a smile and clearly enunciated greeting and the customer told you she was "just looking". The customary reply to Ms. Independent is, "take your time; I'll be right here when you need assistance". You step aside and assist other patrons but later notice that the same customer has been browsing for quite some time. It is perfectly suitable to approach her again before she climbs a ladder that should not be on the floor, to reach an item on the highest shelf because Ms. Independent needs no help, right? Wrong.

Customers are accidents waiting to happen when you turn your back to them. They can be like five year old children, who desperately want to do it all themselves but really need your help. So it is a good idea to check on them routinely. People who never want to be bothered in a store are likely shoplifters; but they cannot steal if you are always paying attention to them. If a person does not want you to do your job then you do not want them in your store.

In this scenario, you have greeted the customers and seated them at the best table in the house. You took their orders and served the meals in perfect time and then they never saw you again until it was time to deliver the check. You never bothered to find out if they enjoyed their meals or to ask if they needed anything, a refill, dessert, nothing.

The guest searching for the server is not an example of good customer service. It means that the guest has noticed something that the server should have been paying closer attention to. The 18% tip you feel inclined to although you have not serviced the guest in over twenty minutes is not going to happen. Your presence *after* their glass is empty and their plate is bare is not up to par.

Sometimes you get busy and we can understand that, but great customer service is when the patron notices how demanding your load is but you still make them feel like they are the only people in the room. Forget the 15% gratuity, now you deserve 20%, and they will return again and again but this time with a larger party; requesting only you.

On the other hand, good customer service as identified in this chapter will also prevent shoplifting. "A recent Newsweek article – "The 'Thrill of Theft': It's not just movie stars. Why, each year, ordinary people shoplift $13 billion of lipsticks, batteries and bikinis from stores" – reported that there are over 800,000 incidents of shoplifting that occur each day in this country. Some retailers even use shoplifting as a guide to taste! "We know what's hot among teens by seeing what they steal," one retail analyst said."[1] How about keeping your eyes open and gauging what they were *about* to steal and thereby get the data and keep the merchandise at the same time. Can you see how it pays to be attentive?

[1] Laurie, Greg, "Who are you when no one is watching?" ,http://www.wnd.com/news/article.asp?ARTICLE_ID=52332

Today's Application:

Your first touch was the greeting. When a customer does not need your assistance immediately, make certain to keep them in your general periphery. In the event that they do take an interest in a product or need your service, you will be there in moment's notice.

Store owners might think of instituting a policy that rewards employees for positively circumventing theft.

> "People will teach you how to sell them if you'll pay attention to the messages they send you." Unknown

_____

notes

eight percent

IT'S NOT PERSONAL

Imagine being at dinner and your date begins having an intense conversation on their cell phone that lasts the entire meal. Rude, huh? Well, the same applies when you are dealing with customers. If your call or conversation with another person is irrelevant to the client in your presence, then do not entertain it. Simply excuse yourself and find a private place to converse; or better yet, call that person back when your client leaves.

Although communication with customers is important, any subject that could paint you or your company in a negative light should be avoided. Profanity and sexual innuendos and harassing remarks are inappropriate at all times. Conversations about what you did last night and with whom, gossip, hot topics about politics and religion have no business in business. In the age of Twitter and Facebook, the compulsion to provide constant updates about what you are doing, at every moment of the day, may seem appropriate but rest assured that your personal pursuits should remain clandestine in the environment of customers. You never want to offend your clientele with meaningless chitchat. It is just not worth the risk.

On the other hand, everything discussed should not be about the product or the service either; in fact you will be hard-pressed to build a relationship with your clients if you never speak of anything beyond the business. Popular television shows and good books are great topics, but the best subject of all is to talk about the customer. There's an idea. Ask them about their life, their family, and their interests. Most customers will engage in that type of dialogue when they know you have a genuine interest and it won't end up being the afternoon gossip. Remember, customer service is about the customer and so should be the context of your conversation.

Today's Application:

Be careful not to let personal matters direct you away from the customer. Be mindful of your conversations and the conversations of your patrons; have you created a pleasing or an unpleasant environment? Finally, drum up a dialogue with a client about something they are always interested in discussing – themselves.

"Conversations should be pleasant without scurrility, witty without

affection, free without indecency, learned without conceitedness, novel without falsehood." William Shakespeare

---

"Loose lips sink ships." American Proverb

---

notes

ON THE HOUSE

If you are authorized to allow people to try something before they buy it, then by all means offer it. This works well with Mr. Undecided. Sampling does two things, it surprises the customer because they are not expecting to get anything for free. Secondly, it increases your likeability, because who does not like *free*. Even if the product was not to their liking, the consumer will not soon forget that you allowed them to try it first. In the event, they really become a fan of the sample; you may have a customer for life.

On a past visit to a Starbucks store in Florida, I attempted to change my palate from coffee to tea. Not a great fan of Chai (then), but desiring a little more than the basic Earl Grey, I stood at the counter bemused. So I asked the barista to tell me more about Rooibus. He offered a dim explanation, so I asked him to compare it to the Chai since that was my real reluctance, and he responded "they are two different types of teas." At that point, I am still blank, remember the product knowledge chapter, I know I did and was wishing that he had taken the course. But to Starbucks' credit there was a wiser barista on staff, and there usually is, if the cashier is not knowledgeable, I can almost guarantee that the barista will be. Anyway, the barista jumped into the conversation and gave me an education in tea lattes that really whet my appetite. Then he added, "try this first one on me, and let me know what you think?" He was so knowledgeable and descriptive with emotion in every word, and he was picking up the tab for my confusion; I had to say "Yes". I appreciated how he massaged my ignorance and allowed me to try the tea. Instantly, I felt better about the service.

In all of my visits to Starbucks, and I have had a plethora, I have never been given anything more than a sample of a seasonal Frappacino. No slight to Starbucks but it is easy to sample something you have already planned to give away; it is another matter to give based on a request or in my case, for demonstration. So after finishing my new favorite drink, I told my new favorite Florida barista that I would be back for more; and I have.

Today's Application:

If you can, offer a genuinely undecided customer an opportunity to sample that product or service. If they like it, great, if it is not their cup of tea, at least they will have

that knowledge. In either scenario, you have helped them to make an informed decision.

ten percent

MAKE A SUGGESTION

Recently I switched to a new cable company. All of the televisions I own are of course cable ready so this was supposed to be a simple deal where you plug the TV in the wall and presto you have picture. Well, no such luck, so I had to call customer service and they told me that they would send a technician right out (great customer service). Well, Joe Blow Cable Guy arrives with a knock loud enough to shake the walls. I open the door and he casually tells me that my cable should be working. He informs me that he did something outside and he proceeds to leave. Knowing how things "should" work and often times do not, I insisted that he come inside and check first – save him another trip and me another call.

Sure enough, I had outdated cables in some of the rooms and there would have been problems. While the original call to the cable company deserved an A+ for quick service, Joe Blow was less than assertive and never would have done anything more than play outside my house had I not suggested that he come in for certainty. His lack of initiative deserved a

D, which combined with the other grade for promptness averaged out to a C for total customer service; just not good enough.

If I have to make my own suggestions, do all the thinking, please tell me what do I need you for?

On another occasion I was out with a friend who had a two day craving for lobster. The dish on the menu would set her back $50 for the lobster lunch. She wanted to make a few changes to the sides, I believe a salad for the potatoes and at first the waiter disapproved based on "restaurant policy." My friend told him to go ask his manager because she really wanted that dish. Well, when he returned with a positive response regarding the salad, I had decided on my own salad – a seafood one for $12. Hearing me question the ingredients in the salad, she begin to ask questions about the salad and decided to get one as well – instead of the lobster. Without any resistance, the waiter changed her order. He did not tell her good the lobster was there and remind her of her self-professed desire and how she might be a little disappointed with the salad because it did not have lobster and she was getting the same greens with her meal anyway. Nothing close to that was said. In this case, I know she would have purchased that lobster but the waiter did not make the suggestion. He obviously did not care if she had a $50, $12, or $0 cost meal, but I bet the owner would.

Dealing with customers is no time to have fear of rejection anxieties. Recall from the previous chapter that this is business, it is not personal. You do not have to take any of your customers home with you so ask, suggest, make a recommendation. Shucks, you work at the place. You ought to know it and its products better than the average customer. Plus, your confidence is refreshing to most patrons. If they deny the recommendation, so be it, but at least you made the effort to surpass their experience and expectations.

Today's Application:

Look for an opportunity to turn a negative into a positive, a lack into lemonade. Make sure the service is complete before ending the conversation.

When you do not have what a customer is looking for, be honest and suggest something of comparable value to try in order to save that customer.

Did your effort to make a suggestion work? If it did, take note of work, if it did not, take note of why not. Either scenario will be a benefit for the next encounter.

notes

eleven percent

DISINFECT

Have you heard of Wendy Whiner? You are not too fond of her, huh? Well, neither are customers. They don't like to hear employees talk behind their boss's back; it makes them uncomfortable. Honestly, what do you want them to do about the fact that you do not like your boss or your job or whatever your objection is about? There is a policy for complaints that should be used. Otherwise, represent the brand you work for and represent yourself, well too by not biting the hand that feeds you.

When a friend and I walked into Subway late one Saturday evening, the store was empty except for a young lady behind the counter, not-so ready to take our order. She did not care to speak or welcome our presence with a smile. Since we were the only ones in line we took our time looking at the above menu until she finally asked, "Do you know what you want?" We decided to try a couple of $5 foot long subs. Very nonchalantly, with no inflection, and no smile, she muttered through the choices of bread and vegetables.

The experience that night was such a poor example of service and one that this leading franchise would be ashamed of. This young lady obviously did not want to work, or so I thought. After she had prepared both subs and was about to ring us up, without asking if we wanted a drink, chips or a cookie; she somehow felt compelled to share her frustrations loud and clear.

"I've been here all day. My stupid a@@ boss put me on the schedule from this morning".

I still don't know why I asked, but curiosity got the best of me and I bit.

"Why? Did someone not show up? " I asked.

She was more than happy to entertain the question.

"Well, I asked him for more hours, but he put me down all day by myself."

With that I took my receipt and sandwich and left dumbfounded. (1) She had a job, (2) She asked for more hours (3) Her boss gave them to her, and (4) She is probably alone because the store is dead. So what's the problem again? Why is she complaining, and furthermore, why is she complaining to us, the customers? She was so wrapped up in her own issues that she never considered that we might be "shopping" the store on behalf of her boss. Although, I chose not to file a complaint, she was a clear candidate to go from more hours to no hours based on her surly attitude and behavior.

Today's Application:

Make sure none of your employees is complaining or displaying a nonchalant demeanor before your customers. If you notice that an employee is upset, carefully remove them from the presence of customers immediately. Bad news spreads like a cold, so you have to ward it off as soon as you notice the symptoms. Once you have the employee alone and away from patrons, ask them if they noticed their conduct. Listen to their answer and then affectively take whatever steps you have in place to assist employees with personal issues.

To employees: No gossip, no disrespect, no personal gripes; just clean casual conversation with and around customers. Today, if you really need to vent, take a moment to excuse yourself and write it down first.

> **"In business - if it doesn't make dollars, then it doesn't make sense."**
> **Unknown**

notes

twelve percent

NEXT PLEASE

This one is self explanatory. Always show a little courtesy to the person who has been waiting the longest. There are lines everywhere these days, and as much as I resent that rope that separates the customer from the check-out area; it makes sense and keeps down confusion.

It was around noon and I decided to visit the local Panera Bread during a very popular time of day. There were four registers open and a line nearly out the door. Everybody's gabbing and waiting their turn in line when the lone dessert cashier decided she would take some of the customers from the sandwich line. Instead of saying "Let me take the next customer in line", she motioned to a good looking fellow near the end of the line, "I can take you over here." As he headed that direction, the irrefutable *next* customer in line went into a rage; she was obviously very hungry and very upset at this cashier's selfish attempt to get a date and lack of consideration for the patrons who had been waiting a long time. She gave that young girl a tongue lashing that she should have expected had she learned the "take the next customer in line" rule during her training. I felt a little sorry for her because that guy she was trying to move to the front of the line did not say a word in her defense. The manager soon arrived on the scene to apologize and began to direct traffic until the lunch rush was over.

In situations like this, where you have cashiers in different areas, I actually prefer the post office's rudimentary take-a-number solution. No one ever has to wonder who is next in line because you have a slip of paper with your number in your hand which coincides with the electronic number on the wall. In the event that someone gets angry, leaves, and gives their number to the guy that just walked in, so be it; the post office did their part to create order.

What would work nicely with their number system is to have more than two people working at a time– that is also a suggestion for Wal-Mart who has neither a rope or a number system; but they did construct the self-service checkout like Publix - where shopping is always a pleasure.

Today's Activity:

If you own or operate a business that has been blessed with customers who will wait in line to get what you have to offer, consider implementing a system that will make that process better and the wait shorter. Find a way to keep down the aggravation that can arise when consumers

have to wait. Until then just take the NEXT customer in line.

thirteen percent

SAY MY NAME
SAY MY NAME

Humans love to hear their names. We are notoriously vain when it comes to the labels our parent's put on us at birth. Instantly we perk up at the sound of it. It is our brand, it distinguishes us from most others. We can hear a stranger use our name, and it instantly triggers us to ask "how do you know me?" Even in a frantic race to our next destination, the sound of our name causes us stop traffic. If ever you want to gain the customer's attention, you can use their name.

After a proper greeting which includes offering your name; most customers will return the welcome. If you have access to their names in your database, always err on the side of using their title and surname before sounding off. If neither of these applies, then create a situation to use their name and then politely ask them to fill in the blank. Whatever you do, when the name is offered, remember it, don't call them by another name. Also, use it sparingly as you would a friend's name in an affable conversation. The overuse of a name can sound redundant and appear contrived.

A business environment is no place for cute little pet names. I am not your "Hun", "sweetie", "girlfriend", or "baby" when I am patronizing your business. Although I understand the lines Shakespeare wrote for Juliet (see quote below), and surely nothing about a customer's genetic makeup will change if they are called by the wrong name, but those terms should be saved for personal relationships; and if you have to wonder about the status of your connection, then you should certainly stay away from those words.

Today's Application:

Make it a goal to use every customer's name at least once during an interaction.

> *Juliet:*
>
> *"What's in a name? That which we call a rose, by any other name would smell as sweet."*

---

fourteen percent

THANK YOU

Sadly, I hear customers saying "thank you" at the end of a transaction more than I hear an employee expressing the same cordiality in return. Maybe they are thanking the person for taking their money, or perhaps they are so quick on the trigger that the employee does not have time to express their gratitude. If that is the case, I hope companies will begin to voice their regards nonetheless and with an emphatic, "No. Thank you, Mr. and Mrs. Customer."

Customers love to hear that they are appreciated. A hand-written thank-you note can add a personal touch every now and then. Hand-written cards work well to provide gratitude and offer a lasting effect. The more professional-personal the card is, the more endearing it will be to the customer. No matter how you choose to express your thanks, a short and sweet word of appreciation makes a happy customer.

Today's Application:

A   simple   "thank   you"   will   do.

fifteen percent

OVERBOOKED and OVERLOOKED

I used to consult with a physician who had a hard time scheduling the length of her treatments because she was unrealistic. Her practice was new, she was dealing with severe cases and she wanted to offer the best care to each patient. However, she had the same battle that most proprietors fight with when it comes to scheduling: client versus profit. The doctor preferred to see lots of patients but she was creating a hostile environment for her staff, especially the receptionist, who was trained to book the appointments an hour and a half apart when they should have been at least two hours per operatory. I advised her that it was worth expanding the appointment if she wanted happy, satisfied clients or she could continue with her current plan, and quickly assume the label "cattle herder" and watch her annoyed patrons find another doctor in this abundantly tourist populated, low-loyalty area. Furthermore, the new schedule allowed her to fit in emergencies. These patients were more than willing to wait when they understood that special allowances were being made to fit them into a busy schedule and the doctor and her staff become the heroes for doing patients a favor versus wasting their time.

Salons like physicians are common perpetrators of overbooking as well. They could really use a continuing education course on how to get clients coiffed and out quickly. Those salons who master the styling and scheduling skills are more profitable than those who do not. It is poor service to take eight hours on a hair cut that isn't even shoulder-length; and to have more than one person scheduled for the same appointment time. Eventually, smart people will leave.

What I have also noticed from most schedule based trades is a fear of losing business. As we know, fear is false evidence appearing real and so is the case for some. They erroneously determine the amount of money they need to make in a day and then base their daily schedule on their net profit. I think that is backwards business thinking and it is not customer-focused and not good customer service. You don't want to treat your client like cattle, herding them in and out every half hour either; you don't want to focus on time at all.

That fear needs to be turned into excitement. Get enthused about giving great service, in the shortest amount of time, to each client. Determine the time requirement for each menu item and give those calculations to the person responsible for scheduling the appointments and watch your clientele grow – happier and larger.

I hear you asking, but what about the cancellations? Yes, I know that it is a critical concern, which is why proprietors are prone to overbook. My suggestion is to implement and enforce a cancellation fee whenever proper notification is not given; and also institute a waiting list. Whatever you do, please avoid penalizing customers for keeping their appointments by making them wait all day.

Today's Application:

Have you been ignoring complaints about the time it is taking your clients to been seen or the length of the visit? Whether you have or you have not, take this time to examine this week's schedule; paying close attention to the days and times that are jam-packed. You may not be able to correct the schedule as it exists today, but promise to discontinue scheduling more than one person for one time and concentrate more on getting clients in and out of the chair. Revisit every service you provide and the times you allow for each; make revisions as needed, discuss this with your staff and start fresh. Review your policy on

cancellations as well, and if you do not have one, take some time to create one.

"You need to be FedEx Fast and Disney Friendly." A.R. Bernard

notes

---

sixteen percent

TAKE YOUR CUES

People like people who are like them. This concept can be challenging because you could appear disingenuous if you take this too far. I am not suggesting that you parrot your client or agree with everything they say. What I do recommend is to respond relative to your client.

For example, if you have a client who talks fast and is always in a rush, you want to step up your game and respond to them in similar fashion. If you did the opposite and began to move slower and drag out your words, you would lose their attention and their business. Get it. You did not become your client, you are not mimicking him or her; you are only speeding up your attention to meet their needs. Conversely, if in that next hour, you meet with a couple and she is a chatty Cathy type and he is a slow Joe in his moving and attention span; you will answer him with brevity and move on while he digests what he's heard, while speaking to his wife with her brand of enthusiasm and lots of explanation. If you try to become them, you will end up with a bipolar disorder, so don't turn into your client, just communicate like them.

Suppose you have difficulty discerning their communication style; then ask "what does good customer service look like to you?" Some customers are very high tech and computer savvy; they want it fast and informal, sent via text or email. Some customers are better with a phone and would rather that you call them. They want the human touch and less technology. Whatever they like is what you should try to exemplify within reason. If you already have certain systems in place using specific telecommunications then gently direct them to the appropriate method.

Here are a few other suggestions for good customer responsive servicing:

- When a customer puts money in your hand, if there is change, place the change back in their hand. The rudest thing you can do is to put their change on the counter. Your body language indicates that you don't want to touch them, although it may not be your intent.

- Make eye contact with your customer. It is a sign of honesty. You want to avoid making them feel uncomfortable, so look them squarely in the eyes.

- When dealing with senior citizens speak as you normally would, unless they ask you to "speak up". It is impolite to automatically assume you need to shout or speak very slow for them to understand.

Assuming anything without the proper cue is discourteous. It only takes a moment to ask before you act.

Today's Activities:

Notice the nonverbal actions of your customers because they are all different. Do they seem to be busy people or are they more relaxed? Are they always on their phones checking emails or responding to text messages? Which ones are very polite? Which ones are very sensitive? Take mental note and try to respond to them based on their personal style. And when in doubt, ask.

notes

seventeen percent

PLAY FAVORITES

Playing favorites or choosing one person over another is usually depicted as a bad thing, even discriminatory, but within the world of customer service it is a necessary opportunity to show long-standing customers that you honor their loyalty.

In this new era where consumers rightfully believe that businesses have lost their devotion to customers, and consumers celebrate the buyer's market; fidelity is a thing of the past. With so many brands and means of purchasing, consumers do not have to patronize one particular label or supplier anymore. The advent of the internet opened up the world to us and changed our paradigms. Losing one customer when there are a plethora via the World Wide Web affected our business relationships. But the basics of business have never changed; consumer and company, buyer and seller, are realizing why they need one another again.   (Revisit tip one and two).

The consumer misses the personalized service and that "Cheers" sensitivity of entering an establishment where everybody knows your name. Consumers are realizing that getting it cheaper is not the sole factor in the decision. They long to talk to a real human, in their own country, when they need assistance. Although some things will never be the same in this global market, and there is no reason why they should be, the company who stands on the principle that retention is more important than new attention will separate them from the rest.

One of the easiest ways to retain customers is to acknowledge their history with your company. I praise the companies who play favorites with lines like "I see Mr. Customer that you have been with us for a quite a few years; Ms. Customer, you are one of our diamond customers and we appreciate your business. Let me take care of that for you right now." Years of service should be recognized and those customers who have been with you from the beginning should be cared for in times of uncertainty not with the strict letter of the law (policy and contracts) but with the spirit of compassion commensurate with their patronage. Something so simple is often blown, by poor hiring decisions, ego, lack of training, and the list goes on, when it cost more money for a company to recapture that lost customer than to keep their favor.

Today's Application:

There are so many things you could do here to reward your loyal customers, but first you should identify when (month and year) your customers began doing business with you. That might take a moment to compile, so get busy.

"Customer service is making the customer feel they are the most important person in the room." Otha Dillihay

notes

eighteen percent

DATE AROUND

Believe it or not, customers like to be romanced, but there are rules to making this an affair to remember. For instance, you never want to be overly aggressive and reveal stalker tendencies. The perfect methodology necessitates a finesse that is best used in the five stages of dating[1]:

The first stage (Attraction) is very simple; they are obviously attracted which is how they found your company. Whatever you did to get them, continue doing it to keep them. Check. Stage One complete.

(Uncertainty) takes the reins in Stage Two. This is normal and fully understandable since they like you, there is an attraction, but you just met; they really do not know you that well. Here is your opportunity to show them they have made the right decision and that you can do the job. Quell their doubts with proof that you are as good as you say you are.

In Stage Three of (Exclusivity), things are maturing well, the relationship is comfortable, you have consistently delivered and they have no thoughts of going anywhere else. There is nothing but smooth sailing tonight.

By the next stage of (Intimacy), the customer is very comfortable with doing business with you. This is the perfect time to get to know them even better through surveys and focus groups. Make them a part of what makes your business a success; share your vision and gain their feedback.

Finally you have them fully (engaged) in your products and/or services in Stage Five. Begin to positively address anything you gleaned about their future needs as determined in stage four. Invite them in (to your world) and create an advocate for your business. Lastly, do not forget to express your gratitude in special, non-solicitous ways.

Today's Application:

Dating a number of people at once is an arduous task, so take your time and just concentrate on the customers that require your attention today. Determine the stage for each, and record and date that information in your customer database. Continue this process until completion.

[1]Mars and Venus on a Date. John Gray, Ph.D., HarperCollins Books. Copyright © 1997.

nineteen percent

PLAN AHEAD

Speaking of dating, how do you know a date has been successful? When they ask you out on another date? In keeping with our Day 18 objective, before you let that customer walk out of the door, let them know you would like to see them again. If you work with appointments, be sure to make the next date before the customer leaves. If your business is not appointment-based, you can ask them "when will we see you again?" I can guarantee you if they were not thinking about coming back before you asked, they are now.

I know a sweet woman, a hairstylist, who has been the long standing beautician for a couple of family members; but she will not schedule an appointment before you leave her shop for the life of her. Failing to put that next date in writing is like letting money walk out of the door. Although there are never any guarantees, at least you have a strong indication that they will be back, particularly if you incorporate the "call before you cancel" policy. Instead she uses her answering machine for bookings. Clients call and leave her a message with the day and time they wish to come in, and when she gets the call in the next day or two, she will call them back to usually say it is confirmed or to offer another time. If she happens to call the client when they are not home, then she leaves a message, and the phone tag begins.

Why make setting an appointment hard? Simple solve: set the appointment when the money is being exchanged. What I have noticed some of her more loyal customers doing before they leave is to pick up the book and schedule their own visit. It is a lazy approach to customer service that has not allowed her the type of growth she should have experienced decades ago. I suggest you book it before it bounces.

Today's Application:

Ask for the next appointment. If this is an existing client, there is likely a pattern already in place, use that knowledge to suggest a date and time. Book it today and cancel those redundant phone calls.

> **"Failing to put that next date in writing is like letting money walk out of the door." Leah Taylor**

twenty percent

GRACE UNDER FIRE

A husband and wife decided to get a little dessert one wintry evening from a restaurant in the local mall. They entered the restaurant about 8:30 pm and the manager who was at the hostess station tells them all the floor seating is closed but they can order from the bar. They obliged, walked to the bar and sat down to order. The bartender asked "What'll you have?" as if he expected them to order drinks. The husband explained that they had a sweet tooth and wanted to get a little dessert. The bartender instantly looked perturbed, not that he was overly friendly before, as he pulled two menus from under the bar and placed them in front of the couple.

The husband who is usually a very social person could not help but notice the dissension and questions his wife, the more cerebral one of the two, "What's wrong with this guy?" She takes a deep breath and shakes her head, hoping for the best. When the bartender returns, the couples select their treats and the turnaround is relatively quick. Things appear to be looking up, but as fate would have it, the husband's hot chocolate is not hot, it is barely warm. The husband motions to the bartender, who is cleaning glasses, and when he arrives the husband explains that his cocoa is barely warm. Without acknowledgement the bartender picks up the mug and walks off. The couple sits there wondering what is going on.

Finally, the husband has hit his limit and decides to confront him. When the bartender returns with a new cocoa, slightly warmer, the husband stands up and asks, "Man, what is your problem? Are you okay?" The bartender condescendingly answers "I don't have a problem."

The husband rebuts, "Yeah, you do. Every since we sat down you have acted like you did not want to serve us. So what's your problem?"

The bartender in a cocky fashion retorts, "No, do you want me to have one?"

Perhaps the bartender had taken a little nip out of one the bottles, but his attitude was distasteful as a server. And to add insult to injury, when the couple tried to reason with the manager, he did not listen but offered to pay their bill and usher them out of the restaurant. "No justice, no peace" were the husband's initial thoughts, but his wife, the writer, quickly calmed that boil to a simmer before things got worse.

The customers wanted the manager to take action and handle the conflict like a professional instead of escorting them out of the restaurant as if they were the trouble-makers. Since the manager failed to listen, the incident was reported to the security company at the mall and submitted to the editorial section of the local paper that week, which did not set well with the owner of the establishment. The owner did take action and two people lost their jobs over warm cocoa. Well, actually you know that is not true. Where there is smoke there is usually fire, this was not the first complaint, only the first to reach this magnitude.

I will not insult your intelligence by suggesting that good customer service is always straightforward. There would be no need for this book if it were. Yes, there are customers from Hell who make it hard to smile and are impossible to satisfy. There are customers who steal, act rude, and mistake your kindness for weakness. These people are their own worst enemies and no one should be fighting for their business. But there are employees who are also belligerent, incorrigible, problematic liars that should never work with the general public and deserve to be terminated immediately before they do further harm to the company. So how do you make that determination when a crisis arises as in this case?

The first step is to isolate the problem and the parties involved to establish what happened without further argument. Get only the facts and begin with the customer. Let them know that you will be speaking with that employee, but your primary concern is to make sure that you hear their side of the story first. Take the appropriate time to hear the complaint (Day 6). You want to also make the proper notification of the incident in order to address the customer's problem with a proper solution. At this juncture, the worst thing a company can do is to attempt a defense for an employee's actions. You might as well call the customer a liar. To an already offended customer, a rebuttal does not amount to a hill of beans and only serves to stir the pot. Your job is to put out fires, not start new ones.

You never want to rush to judgment instead show empathy. That does not mean that you cave in on a ridiculous request or change your policies and procedures, your only job is to listen. And repeat what they say for accuracy and clear understanding. This leads to the third and final step, which is to offer the solution.

What does matter is the company's bottom line and how this will affect other customers. Settling this in the newspaper is not good for the business; settle it before the patron leaves, and try to make sure they leave with some level of satisfaction. Offer a resolution in the form of a question, to make sure you are satisfying the customer's concerns, and have gained their buy-in.

The restaurant in question did not do any of this. They did not even note the incident for their own records and it came back to bite them.

Today's Application:

Bad things happen, even to good people and good companies. Make sure you have procedures in place to handle crisis situations. Exercise empathy, note everything and be prepared to offer a solution. Avoidance is not an answer.

notes

twenty-one percent

PRACTICE MAKES A HABIT

At this point you probably have noticed that these steps to better customer service are quite simple. They always have been. At the core, customer service is about knowing your roles and your goals and not deviating from what works. Your role Is to serve and represent a company during office hours. Your goal is to provide customer satisfaction so they will keep coming back for more. When you deviate and get out of your lane for whatever reason, the level of service suffers and the ability to increase profits diminishes.

Somewhere in the atmosphere, we, as humans made this difficult and turned the customer into the bad guy. Today will hopefully signify a change in that type of combative thinking and behavior. Today is the day to commit to continuing in the practice of good, better and eventually, great customer service.

In all fairness, whether the customer is sweet as pie or rotten to the core matters not. Your primary goal and role is to remain consistent. The book of Proverbs speaks of "unfair scales and measures" and the results. Your job is not to dish out a certain type of service for certain types of customers, it is to serve all mankind, and that service ought to be your best. It should be a part of your mission and your vision statement. Again, your position is to remain consistent in providing great service regardless.

Now once the service has been provided and you decide that you do not want to continue servicing a tyrant of a customer because they are turning off all the other customers, then there is a courteous way to deliver that bit of news as well. Send me an email at leah@reallyleah.com for more information.

Today's Application:

Make the daily principles in this book a daily practice and watch your business prosper.

Dear Business Owner,

When your profits begin to increase because of the tips shared in this book, please allow me to celebrate in your good fortune. Simply visit my website, **www.ReallyLeah.com** and post your comments.

Sincerely,

Leah

100% bonus chapter

GET THE SERVICE
YOU DESERVE

There are two main reasons an angelic customer like you is not getting the service you deserve and neither has anything to do with those devils at that big bad store. Of course, I am joking, but only slightly. There really are two primary explanations for some of the dissatisfaction you experience and we will explore what you can do to empower yourself.

The first reason customers do not get the service they desire is due to a dangerous case of apathy concerning customer service. Customers often complain about their service but they refuse to take the action steps needed to make a difference. Humans innately have this fear of not being liked or being vilified if they take up for themselves so they shy away from getting involved. Their conversations and complaints never go beyond their circle of friends, and even if they do voice them to the person violating basic customer service rules, those same concerns never make it to the person in authority with the power to create change. Others fear confrontation to the extent that they would allow a contractor to drive a steamroller through their front door and they would simply wave, "hello." Bully companies with bully customer service representatives eat these guys up for lunch. If you are this person, you have to become assertive; you will have to learn to speak up, and learn to follow the steps at the end of this chapter.

> **"You want something but don't get it. You kill and covet, but you cannot have what you want. You quarrel and fight. You do not have because you do not ask God." James (4:2)**

The second reason a customer will get lousy service is because they can dish it out but cannot take it. Truth be told, they swim in the mainstream of hypocrisy where they ultimately get what they give. The only consistency in their life is their desire to be right all the time and in every situation. When asked, is the customer always right? Their answer is a biased, "yes" and "no." The answer is yes, if they are the customer, and the answer is no, whenever they are not. BOMP! Wrong answer. The truth they neglect is that the customer is always right until and unless proven otherwise. And no business should be in the business of proving customers wrong for the sake of being right.

This selfish consumer who overacts about everything and hates all service personnel is typically the selfish service-provider who lacks people skills and hates their job. If this is true, you need to take a long look in a mirror. Get a clue. It is not all about you. If that truth hurts, it is only because it is the truth. The amazing thing is that this ugly truth has an easy fix that begins and ends with you. Stop being a self-centered person. When you begin to treat people like you want to be treated, you will inevitably perceive that people are treating you better because good service is what you will attract.

"Be the change you want to see in the world." Gandhi

---

7 STEPS TO THE
SERVICE YOU DESERVE:

1. Show Confidence. Say what you mean and mean what you say. Be direct and to the point and expect favorable results.

2. Be friendly. You are serious about what you are saying but you do not have to look, sound or act ugly. We reap what we sow.

3. Point it out. If the company makes a mistake, share the mistake, politely. People cannot learn from mistakes if you are busy covering them. A mistake in customer service is a powerful learning opportunity. We all make mistakes and it helps us to grow. Do not take that away from someone. Allow them to do their job – the correct way.

4. Use equal scales. Share your good experiences as well as the bad ones. This is an excellent way to not feel like the "bad guy." When you can honestly say that you are always giving credit where it is due; that you give more compliments than you give complaints; you can rest assured that you are fair in your assessments.

5. Handle it immediately. Don't let the sun go down on your anger. If you have a serious complaint, speak to a manager as soon possible, without emotion but facts. While the details are fresh, amass your evidence and state your case.

6. Take notes. Remember your expectation is to receive great customer service, which means you will want to share that with someone in the company. So always at the beginning of a transaction take time to note the name of the person with

whom you are speaking. Record the date and time of your conversations if they are not on your invoice, along with any pertinent information or promises made. Keep those notes in a safe place where you can easily retrieve them for that all impressive compliment or for that unavoidable complaint.

7. Resolve it. Have a solution in mind before presenting the problem. Good customer service agents will often turn the question to you, the consumer, and ask what you would like to be done to rectify the error or problem, and you need to have an answer, in fact a highly plausible one is needed, if you want to be taken seriously. Usually the crime should fit the punishment - an eye for an eye - so make sure your desired resolution is something comparable to the damage. If the service did not put your life at risk then you should not try to sue someone and take away their life's blood. That is not what this chapter is about. Again, accidents and mistakes happen. Sometimes an apology will suffice. Whatever the case, use good judgment and offer a wise solution when asked.

"Do unto others as you would have them do unto you." Jesus Christ (Luke 6:31)

Dear Customer,

When you begin to get the service you deserve, based on the information presented in this chapter, and you decide to resuscitate your hard earned tip and patronage, please let me know about it so I can share it with others. Post your good news and comments on my website, **www.ReallyLeah.com.** I look forward to hearing from you. **Prosperity to all.**

Sincerely,

Leah